The Christian and the Abundant Life

Focusing on New Priorities

STEP 2

Bill Bright

NewLife
PUBLICATIONS
A MINISTRY OF CAMPUS CRUSADE FOR CHRIST

Ten Basic Steps Toward Christian Maturity
Step 2: The Christian and the Abundant Life

Published by
New*Life* Publications
100 Sunport Lane
Orlando, FL 32809

Printed in the United States of America.

ISBN: 1-56399-031-8

Thomas Nelson Inc., Nashville, Tennessee, is the exclusive distributor of this book to the trade markets in the United States and the District of Columbia.

Distributed in Canada by Campus Crusade for Christ of Canada, Surrey, B.C.

Unless otherwise indicated, all Scripture references are from the *New International Version*, © 1973, 1978, 1984 by the International Bible Society. Published by Zondervan Bible Publishers, Grand Rapids, Michigan.

Scripture quotations designated TLB are from *The Living Bible,* © 1971 by Tyndale House Publishers, Wheaton, Illinois.

Scripture quotations designated NKJ are from the *New King James* version, © 1979, 1980, 1982 by Thomas Nelson Inc., Publishers, Nashville, Tennessee.

Any royalties from this book or the many other books by Bill Bright are dedicated to the glory of God and designated to the various ministries of Campus Crusade for Christ/*NewLife2000*.

For more information, write:

L.I.F.E.—P. O. Box 40, Flemmington Markets, 2129, Australia
Campus Crusade for Christ of Canada—Box 300, Vancouver, B.C., V6C 2X3, Canada
Campus Crusade for Christ—Fairgate House, King's Road, Tyseley, Birmingham, B11 2AA, England
Lay Institute for Evangelism—P. O. Box 8786, Auckland 3, New Zealand
Campus Crusade for Christ—Alexandra, P. O. Box 0205, Singapore 9115, Singapore
Great Commission Movement of Nigeria—P. O. Box 500, Jos, Plateau State Nigeria, West Africa
Campus Crusade for Christ International—100 Sunport Lane, Orlando, FL 32809, USA

Contents

Acknowledgments 4

A Personal Word 5

What This Study Will Do for You 7

How to Use This Study 10

Living the Abundant Life 13

LESSONS

   1 ❖ What Is the Christian Life? 19

   2 ❖ Appraising Your Spiritual Life 27

   3 ❖ Living Abundantly 31

   4 ❖ The Abiding Life 37

   5 ❖ The Cleansed Life 43

   6 ❖ Victorious in Spiritual Warfare 49

   7 ❖ Attitude Makes the Difference 55

   8 ❖ Recap 60

Resources to Help You Live Abundantly 62

Acknowledgments

The *Ten Basic Steps Toward Christian Maturity* series was a product of necessity. As the ministry of Campus Crusade for Christ expanded rapidly to scores of campuses across America, thousands of students committed their lives to Christ—several hundred on a single campus. Individual follow-up of all new converts soon became impossible. Who was to help them grow in their new-found faith?

A Bible study series designed for new Christians was desperately needed—a study that would stimulate individuals and groups to explore the depths and the riches of God's Word. Although several excellent studies were available, we felt the particular need of new material for these college students.

In 1955, I asked several of my fellow staff associates to assist me in the preparation of Bible studies that would stimulate both evangelism and Christian growth in a new believer. The contribution by campus staff members was especially significant because of their constant contact with students in introducing them to Christ and meeting regularly with them to disciple them. Thus, the *Ten Basic Steps Toward Christian Maturity* was the fruit of our combined labor.

Since that modest beginning, many other members of the staff have contributed generously. On occasion, for example, I found myself involved in research and writing sessions with several of our staff, all seminary graduates, some with advanced degrees and one with his doctorate in theology. More important, all were actively engaged in "winning, building, and sending men" for Christ.

For this latest edition, I want to thank Don Tanner for his professional assistance in revising, expanding, and editing the contents. I also want to thank Joette Whims and Jean Bryant for their extensive help and for joining Don and me in the editorial process.

A Personal Word

I have a reputation for being an optimist. A friend once said to me, "Bill you're unbelievable. Doesn't anything ever get you down?" Well, I have my moments like everyone else when I am tempted and discouraged. But one of the greatest lessons I have learned through the years is to give praise to my Lord in all things—in trials as well as triumphs.

And I do have my fair share of trials. Frankly, the fleshly part of me can get discouraged—sometimes upset—in the face of adversity. My sinful nature can still cause trouble. Without Christ in control of my life, my outlook and demeanor would be anything but cheerful. But as I have grown in the Lord and allowed Him to guide me through His Spirit, His supernatural joy and peace have become more and more a part of me.

I have discovered that the more I praise my heavenly Father, meditate on His wonderful Word, walk in the power of the Holy Spirit, and talk with others about Jesus, the less my natural side influences my attitudes and actions. When the living Christ controls my life, I do not have to struggle to be joyful and calm in my own strength; the Spirit of God pours out an ample supply of optimism from within so that generally my first reaction to adversity is one of genuine joy and peace.

Jesus said, "I came that they might have life, and might have it abundantly" (John 10:10, TLB). Many Christians today believe that, after receiving Christ as Savior and Lord, their ultimate salvation and favor with God depends on keeping a long list of *got-to's* and *can't-do's*. As a result, their lives become filled with self-righteous bitterness that wells up and spews out of them in the form of judgmental, negative, defeatist attitudes. The secret to victorious living, however, lies not in keeping a long litany of rules and regulations, but in developing an intimate, personal, vital love relationship with our Lord Jesus Christ.

Jesus is the visible expression of the invisible God (Colossians 1:15). In Him "the fullness of the Deity lives in bodily form" (Colossians 2:9). God has given Jesus "all authority in heaven and on earth" (Matthew 28:18), and we are "complete in Him" (Colossians 2:10, NKJ). When we link our weak, finite lives up with His supernatural life, we begin to live a new quality of life altogether. We exchange our lives of defeat, frustration, and fruitlessness for His life of victory, joy, and peace. Being filled with His Spirit and daily walking hand in hand with our Lord in His supernatural power is the key to experiencing the abundant life.

It is my prayer that this study will bless and enrich your life in a supernatural way and help you to fully experience what God has in store for you—a life that is truly abundant and without equal.

Bill Bright

What This Study Will Do for You

I remember well that night in 1944 when, alone in my home, I knelt to surrender my will to Christ. Although I felt no great emotional response, as some have, Christ came into my life—true to His promise (Revelation 3:20).

Gradually, like the blooming of a lovely rose, the beauty and fragrance of His presence became real to me. Although I thought I was perfectly happy and challenged with life as a non-believer, Jesus gave me a new quality of life altogether—an abundant life fulfilled in ways too numerous to mention.

This practical study, prepared especially for you, will help you experience this abundant life also.

Step 2: The Christian and the Abundant Life describes the Christian way of life—what it is and how it works practically. This study discusses problems of temptation, sin, and spiritual warfare. The principles you are about to study will help you evaluate your walk with the Lord. They will point you toward the path of Christian victory and the abundant life.

You will benefit from this study in two ways:

First, *you will gain a better understanding of the abundant life.*

Men and women by the thousands have been used of God to change history as God used His Word to change them.

Many Christians are defeated and frustrated simply because they do not know what the Bible says about the victory that is ours through Christ as we live lives of faith and obedience.

The psalmist says, "The entrance of your words gives light" (Psalm 119:130), and Jesus taught that "the truth will set you free" (John 8:32).

I assure you that if you apply the proven concepts presented in this study, you will discover the dynamic new life available only through Jesus Christ. And you will become a more victorious, radiant witness for our Lord.

Second, *God's power will change your life.*

Hebrews 4:12 proclaims:

> The word of God is living and active. Sharper than any double-edged sword, it penetrates even to dividing soul and spirit...it judges the thoughts and attitudes of the heart.

Men and women by the thousands—including Martin Luther, C. S. Lewis, Billy Graham, and many others—have been used of God to change history as God used His Word to change them. As you study this material, you will undoubtedly sense changes taking place in your life, too. And you will gain a greater awareness of God's power in your life.

Foundation for Faith

Step 2: The Christian and the Abundant Life is part of the *Ten Basic Steps Toward Christian Maturity,* a time-tested study series designed to provide you with a sure foundation for your faith. Hundreds of thousands have benefited from this Bible study series during the almost forty years since it was first published in its original form.

When you complete Step 2, I encourage you to continue your study with the rest of the Steps.

If you are a new Christian, the *Ten Basic Steps* will acquaint you with the major doctrines of the Christian faith. By applying the principles you learn, you will grow spiritually and find solutions to problems you are likely to face as a new believer.

If you are a mature Christian, you will discover the tools you need to help others receive Christ and grow in their faith. Your own commitment to our Lord will be affirmed, and you will discover how to develop an effective devotional and study plan.

The series includes an individual booklet for the introductory study and one for each of the ten Steps. These study guides correlate with the expanded and updated *Handbook for Christian Maturity* and *Ten Basic Steps Leader's Guide.*

Each Step reveals a different facet of the Christian life and truth, and each contains lessons for study that can be used during your personal quiet times or in a group setting.

I encourage you to pursue the study of Step 2 with an open, eager mind. As you read, continually pray that God will show you how to apply the principles you learn to your own situation on a daily basis, and you will make the wonderful discovery of the abundant, Spirit-filled life.

How to Use This Study

On page 13 of this Step, you will find the preparatory article, "Living the Abundant Life." The article will give you a clear perspective on how to live the abundant life. Read it carefully before you begin Lesson 1. Review it prayerfully during your study.

This step contains seven lessons plus a "Recap" or review. Each lesson is divided into two sections: the Bible Study and the Life Application. Begin by noting the Objective for the lesson you are studying. The Objective states the main goal for your study. Keep it in mind as you continue through the lesson.

Take time to memorize the referenced Scripture verses. Learn each verse by writing it on a small card to carry with you. You can buy cards for these verses at any bookstore or print shop, or you can make your own by using filing cards. Review daily the verses you have memorized.

Our Lord has commanded that we learn His Word. Proverbs 7:1–3 reminds us:

> My son, keep my words and store up my commands within you. Keep my commands and you will live; guard my teachings as the apple of your eye. Bind them on your fingers; write them on the tablet of your heart.

As you meditate on the verses you have memorized and claim God's promises, you will experience the joy, victory, and power

As you apply the verses you have memorized, you will experience the joy, victory, and power that God's Word gives you.

that God's Word gives to your Christian walk. When you have finished all the studies in the entire series, you will be able to develop your own Bible study, continuing to use a systematic method for memorizing God's Word.

How to Study the Lessons

Casual Bible reading uncovers valuable spiritual facts that lie near the surface. But understanding the deeper truths requires study. Often the difference between reading and studying is a pen and notepad.

Every lesson in this study covers an important topic and gives you an opportunity to record your answers to the questions. Plan to spend a minimum of thirty minutes each day—preferably in the morning—in Bible study, meditation, and prayer.

Remember, the most important objective and benefit of a quiet time or Bible study is not to acquire knowledge or accumulate biblical information but to meet with God in a loving, personal way.

Here are some suggestions to help you in your study time:

◆ Plan a specific time and place to work on these studies. Make an appointment with God; then keep it.

◆ Use a pen or pencil, your Bible, and this booklet.

◆ Begin with prayer for God's presence, blessing, and wisdom.

◆ Meditate on the Objective to determine how it fits into your circumstances.

◆ Memorize the suggested verses.

◆ Proceed to the Bible study, trusting God to use it to teach you. Prayerfully anticipate His presence with you. Work carefully, reading the Scripture passages and thinking through the questions. Answer each as completely as possible.

◆ When you come to the Life Application, answer the questions honestly and begin to apply them to your own life.

◆ Prayerfully read through the lesson again and reevaluate your Life Application answers. Do they need changing? Or adjusting?

◆ Review the memory verses.

◆ Consider the Objective again and determine if it has been accomplished. If not, what do you need to do?

◆ Close with a prayer of thanksgiving, and ask God to help you grow spiritually in the areas He has specifically revealed to you.

◆ When you complete the first seven lessons of this Step, spend extra time on the Recap to make sure you understand every lesson thoroughly.

◆ If you need more study of this Step, ask God for wisdom again and go through whatever lesson(s) you need to review, repeating the process until you do understand and are able to apply the truths to your own life.

These studies are not intended as a complete development of Christian beliefs. However, a careful study of the material will give you, with God's help, a sufficient understanding of how you can know and apply God's plan for your life. The spiritual truths contained here will help you meet with our Lord Jesus Christ in an intimate way and discover the full and abundant life that Jesus promised (John 10:10).

Do not rush through the lessons. Take plenty of time to think through the questions. Meditate on them. Absorb the truths presented, and make the application a part of your life. Give God a chance to speak to you, and let the Holy Spirit teach you. As you spend time with our Lord in prayer and study, and as you trust and obey Him, you will experience the amazing joy of His presence (John 14:21).

Living the Abundant Life

Did you know that an estimated 400,000 young people will attempt to take their lives this year, and that as many as 15,000 will likely succeed?

What a terrible tragedy that so many no longer consider life worth living!

No doubt drugs and the despair reflected in many of today's songs, books, and movies add to the emotional climate that prompts such self-destruction.

What is it that drives so many young people to give up on life? When teens who made the "Who's Who in High Schools" were asked what their greatest fear was, 80 percent answered, "The fear of failure."

Such sobering statistics remind me of a statement recorded in God's Word:

> We need have no fear of someone who loves us perfectly; his perfect love for us eliminates all dread of what he might do to us. If we are afraid, it is for fear of what he might to do us, and shows that we are not fully convinced that he really loves us (1 John 4:18, TLB).

Let me ask you, are you living a joyous and abundant life for the Lord Jesus, or is your life filled with anxiety and fear?

With God "life is an endless hope," and without God "life is a hopeless end."

Let me share with you three principles that will help you live an abundant life and enable you to be a fruitful witness for our Lord.

Develop a Lasting Relationship

The first principle is to *develop a deep and lasting relationship with our Lord.*

When Valerie had to undergo chemotherapy and radiation for several months, Brenda took over the grocery shopping and house cleaning. At first Valerie felt embarrassed when her best friend scrubbed the kitchen floor or scoured the bathrooms. But as Valerie lost more of her strength and had extensive surgery, Brenda's selfless loving care began to seem more beautiful.

Many months later, when Valerie had recovered and her medical tests came back free of cancer cells, Brenda was the one Valerie celebrated with. She took her friend out to dinner at an exclusive restaurant. They laughed and joked. But before they left the table, Valerie handed Brenda a small notebook filled with hand-written notes.

"All during my treatment," Valerie said, "I wrote down what your encouragement and help meant to me. Please read this whenever you feel discouraged."

Brenda flipped to the last page in the notebook. In bold letters was written "Thanks for your Christ-like spirit. I love you. Valerie."

Deep and lasting friendships make our lives more complete, fulfilling, and worthwhile. We have all learned to invest time and energy in these relationships to keep them healthy and strong. But what could be more rewarding than to nurture a personal and intimate relationship with our wonderful Lord Jesus Christ?

Anyone who studies God's holy Word can gain intellectual knowledge about God. But one must receive Jesus Christ as his personal Savior and Lord to really have an intimate relationship with Him.

In 2 Peter 1:2 we read, "Grace and peace be yours in abundance through the knowledge of God and of Jesus our Lord." When we receive the Lord Jesus Christ as our personal Savior, we receive His grace. This grace, or unmerited favor of God, is always accompanied by peace—a quiet, inner calm that assures us of His presence and power in our lives.

When we receive Christ, we are cleansed from every sin, and the Lord Jesus presents us to His Father pure and holy, without spot or blemish. His gift of purity and our love for Him inspire us to keep His commandments and as a result enjoy a life of fruitfulness.

"No branch can bear fruit by itself; it must remain in the vine," our Lord said. "Neither can you bear fruit unless you remain in me" (John 15:4). As we surrender the control of our lives completely to Him, His Holy Spirit flows through us. We find ourselves overflowing with joy, and the love of God compels us to share His love and forgiveness with others as a way of life.

Place God at the Center

The second principle is to *place God at the center of your hopes and plans.*

Someone has said that with God "life is an endless hope" and without God "life is a hopeless end."

God is the author of life—both physical and spiritual. He alone, through the blood of His Son, Jesus Christ, can remove the guilt of our past. He alone, through the power of the Holy Spirit, can give us the strength to cope with the problems of our present. He alone, through the assurance of His holy Word, can give us the faith to face the future with confidence.

Bear Fruit

The third principle is to *bear fruit.*

I like the words of the apostle Paul recorded in 1 Corinthians 15:10, "By the grace of God, I am what I am." A key to bearing fruit is a positive self-image built on the foundation of God's love and grace. This will enable us to more effectively share Christ and be a fruitful spiritual multiplier for our Lord.

Part of the fruit-bearing process is to love others. Our Lord boiled down all of life into two great commandments:

Love the Lord your God with all your heart, soul,
and mind.

and

Love your neighbor as much as you love yourself.

Someone has said that unless you love God, you will perish
spiritually; unless you accept yourself, you will perish emotionally;
and unless you love others, you will perish socially. It is vital that
those with whom we share the Lord Jesus sense our love and
acceptance of them, or they will not receive our witness or compre-
hend God's great love for them.

Living With Purpose

The Christian life is one of victory, joy, peace, and purposeful living.
Jesus said, "The thief does not come except to steal, and to kill, and
to destroy. I have come that they may have life, and that they may
have it more abundantly" (John 10:10).

Although many professing Christians are living in defeat and
discouragement, this is not the New Testament norm. Picture the
apostles Paul and Silas imprisoned in Philippi. They were beaten
and cast into the inner prison where their feet were locked in the
stocks. Yet they prayed and sang praises to God. Their confidence
was not in themselves. Their trust was in the true living God whom
they loved, worshiped, and served.

Picture, too, the disciples and thousands of other first-century
Christians singing praises to God as they were burned at the stake,
crucified, or fed to the lions. They faced horrible deaths with
courage and joy because of their vital, personal relationship with
Christ. Many have seen friends and relatives for whom they prayed
invite Jesus to be Savior and Lord. Others have overcome destruc-
tive habits and attitudes to experience joy and confidence.

Down through the centuries, there have been—and still are—
hundreds of millions of Christians who have dedicated their very
lives to Christ and have enjoyed the abundant life Christ promised.

You may not find it necessary to die for Christ, but are you will-
ing to live for Him? Andrew Murray, author of many Christian
classics, wrote:

The low state of the spiritual life of Christians is due to the fact that they do not realize that the aim and object of conversion is to bring the soul, even here on earth, to a daily fellowship with the Father in heaven. When once this truth has been accepted, the believer will perceive how indispensable it is to the spiritual life of a Christian to take time each day with God's Word and in prayer to wait upon God for His presence and His love to be revealed.

It is not enough at conversion to accept forgiveness of sins, or even to surrender to God. That is only a beginning. The young believer must understand that he has no power of his own to maintain his spiritual life. No, he needs each day to receive new grace from heaven through fellowship with the Lord Jesus.

This cannot be obtained by a hasty prayer, nor a superficial reading of a few verses from God's Word. He must take time quietly and deliberately to come into God's presence, to feel his own weakness and his need, and to wait upon God through His Holy Spirit, to renew the heavenly light and life in his heart. Then he may rightly expect to be kept by the power of Christ throughout the day, with all its temptations.

Many of God's children long for a better life, but do not realize the need of giving God time day by day in their inner chamber through His Spirit to renew and sanctify their lives.

Meditate on this thought: The feeble state of my spiritual life is mainly due to the lack of time day by day in fellowship with God.

I encourage you to come joyfully into our Lord's presence today and every day. Find a quiet place where you can be alone and fellowship with God by reading and meditating on His holy, inspired Word. Discover what His Word has to say about your life. Experience the abundant life for which He created you. Then take the initiative to share the Lord Jesus Christ and the blessings that He offers with your loved ones, neighbors, and friends.

What Is the Christian Life?

The Christian life begins with receiving the Lord Jesus Christ—the gift of God's love and forgiveness—by faith. It results in a threefold commitment to a person, the person of the Lord Jesus Christ. It is a commitment to Him of your intellect, emotions, and will.

The Christian life is a personal, intimate relationship between you and Christ. This life begins in faith (Ephesians 2:8,9) and can only be lived by faith. Faith is another word for trust. We trust our lives to Christ's keeping because He has proven Himself trustworthy by His life, His death, His resurrection, and His abiding presence—His unconditional love.

❖

Objective: To understand our new life in Christ and how to begin growing

Read: John 1–3

Memorize: 2 Corinthians 5:17

As you walk in faith and obedience to God as an act of your will and allow Him to change your life, you will gain increasing assurance of your relationship with Him. You will experience God's work in your life as He enables you to do what you cannot do on your own.

Bible Study

A New Creation

1. On the basis of 2 Corinthians 5:17, what has happened to you? *THE OLD DON HAS DIED, I AM A NEW CREATION*

What are some evidences in your life of new things having come, and old things having passed away?

NEW THINGS THAT HAVE COME	OLD THINGS THAT HAVE PASSED AWAY
FAITH *FAMILY (CHRISTIAN)* *LOVE* *SALVATION, (ASSURED)* *DIRECTION* *HUMILITY (PRAYING FOR)* *MEEKNESS*	*I DO NOT WISH TO ANSWER THESE AT THIS TIME, BUT REST ASSURED GOD IS ELIMINATING ALL THE "DROSS", SUCH AS ANGER, ENVY, SELFISHNESS, GOSSIP, SLANDER. DRUGS + ALCOHOL*

2. To what does the Bible compare this experience of newness (John 3:3)? *THAT WE CANNOT + WILL NOT EXPERIENCE GOD'S KINGDOM UNLESS A new birth*

Compare the experience of physical birth with spiritual birth. What are the similarities? *— A NEW BEGINNING, AMAZEMENT, AT THE WORLD, LEARNING TO "CRAWL" (SPIRITUAL GROWTH) BEFORE you CAN WALK (SPIRITUAL MATURITY) RELATIONSHIPS (FELLOWSHIP)*

3. How was your new birth accomplished (John 3:16; 1:12,13)?

GOD GAVE HIS SON AS ATONING SACRIFICE FOR OUR SINS, WHEN WE ACCEPT + BELIEVE

4. According to Ephesians 2:8,9, what did you do to merit this gift? *BELIEVE AND HAVE FAITH*

Why is this so important to our spiritual well-being?

BECAUSE WE ARE JUSTIFIED BY FAITH, AND GROW ACCORDINGLY

5. Colossians 1:13,14 speaks of two kingdoms. Describe the nature of each kingdom in relation to your life before and after you received Christ. *— BEFORE MY SALVATION I WAS ENTRENCHED IN DRUGS, ANGER, STRIFE, GREED + ALCOHOL, MY NEW KINGDOM IS FILLED WITH LOVE, PATIENCE, KINDNESS AND IS CHRIST CENTERED. Amen! Praise the Lord!*

A New Relationship With God

1. What are you called (1 Peter 2:2)?

NEWBORN BABIES

What should be your desire? *PURE SPIRITUAL MILK*

2. What is your new relationship with God (John 1:12)?

I AM A CHILD OF GOD!

3. What does it mean to you to be a partaker of the divine nature (2 Peter 1:4)? *THAT WE WILL HAVE THE CHARACTER OF CHRIST*

4. How do you know that you are God's child (Galatians 4:6; Romans 8:16)? *- BECAUSE GOD GAVE US HIS HOLY SPIRIT*

A New Motivation

1. How does the love of Christ motivate you (2 Corinthians 5:14,15)? *THAT MY LIFE IS NOT MY OWN I AM CHRISTS and when I see how much Christ sacrificed for me I want to live for Him!*

2. What has replaced self as the most important factor (verse 15)? *CHRIST CENTERED LIFE*

   My love for Jesus

3. What two things have happened in your life to give you new motivation, according to Colossians 3:1–4?

   1) *YOUR HEART ON THINGS ABOVE*

   2) *YOUR MIND ON THINGS ABOVE*

   What has happened to your old life according to verse 3?
   IT IS DEAD

   What will motivate you to seek those things that are above, according to verse 1? *A HEART AND MIND THAT IS CHRIST CENTERED*

What is the promise we are given (verse 4)? How does it affect your motivation? *THAT AT THE COMING OF OUR LORD AND SAVIOR WE WILL BE GLORIFIED w/ HIM IT IS THE MEANS BY WHICH I TRY TO LIVE MY LIFE*

A New Relationship With Mankind

1. What is new about your relationship with people (1 John 3:11,14)? *– THAT WE SHOULD LOVE ONE ANOTHER.*

2. How can you show that you are a follower of Christ (John 13:35)? *– By LOVING ALL MEN, PEOPLE will SEE + KNOW THAT WE ARE FOLLOWERS OF CHRIST*

In what ways are you doing this in your everyday life? *WHERE I'M AT THIS SOMETIMES IS VERY HARD TO DO, SO I FIND MYSELF PRAYING CONSTANTLY, I TREAT EVERYONE W/ RESPECT AND ALSO ASK FOR MEN'S PRAYER REQUESTS. I HAVE SEEN MANY PRAYERS ANSWERED*

3. Read 2 Corinthians 5:18–21. Describe the ministry that has been given to you. *THE MINISTRY OF RECONCILIATION THAT IS THE SPREADING OF THE GOOD NEWS OF JESUS CHRIST*

We are called *AMBASSADORS* for Christ (verse 20). In what ways are you fulfilling your call? *I CONSTANTLY PRAY FOR OPPORTUNITIES TO WITNESS + TESTIFY TO NOT ONLY GOD'S GOSPEL MESSAGE, BUT ALSO TO WHAT HE HAS DONE FOR ME.*

4. As a follower of Christ, what is the greatest thing you can do (Matthew 4:19)? *TO WITNESS FOR JESUS CHRIST, SPREAD THE "GOOD NEWS"*

Be a fisher of man!

Name at least three ways you can do that in your own life.

1) *AT WORK TO FELLOW EMPLOYEES, NEIGHBOR*

2) *TO STRANGERS WE MEET ON THE STREET, OR PEOPLE WHO WE KNOW ARE LOST*

3) *TO MEN WHO YOU ARE SURROUNDED BY EVERY DAY (PRISON) BY YOUR WORD, DEED + ACTIONS*

5. How can your friends benefit from the message you deliver to them (1 John 1:3,4)? *FIRST BY COMING TO THE KNOWLEDGE AND SAVING GRACE OF JESUS CHRIST THROUGH YOUR WITNESSING AND LIFE,*

SECOND IT IS HARD TO IGNORE A CHANGED LIFE,

THIRD THROUGH YOUR PRAYERS, THAT THE HOLY SPIRIT MAY CONSTANTLY CONVICT THEM

LIFE APPLICATION

1 What is the greatest change you have seen in your life since you became a new creation in Christ Jesus?

WHEN I AM OBEDIENT, I SEE THAT "ALL THINGS" WORK FOR GOOD FOR THOSE WHO LOVE THE LORD" - THAT GOD BLESSES ME, AND REMOVES THE "DROSS" & IS REFINING ME

2 In your new relationship with God, what now can be your response toward problems, disappointments, and frustrations (1 Peter 5:7; Romans 8:28)?

I CAST ALL MY ANXIETIES ON HIM BECAUSE HE CARES FOR ME

3 How will you change your goals as a result of your new motivation?

MY GOAL IS TO HAVE A LIFE THAT IS "GOD CENTERED" TO PUT WORLDLY THINGS ASIDE AND KNOW THAT HE IS IN CONTROL

4 What is your responsibility now to other men and women? How will you carry it out?

MY FOREMOST RESPONSIBILITY IS TO PREACH CHRIST CRUCIFIED FOR ALL MEN. MY HOPE IS TO ACCOMPLISH THIS THROUGH THE PRISON MINISTRY, AND WHOEVER GOD SENDS MY WAY

5 List two changes you would like to see in your life now that you are a Christian. Ask God to bring about those changes.

1) *HUMILITY*

2) *MEEKNESS*

Appraising Your Spiritual Life

The two circles in the diagram below represent two kinds of lives: the self-directed life and the Christ-directed life.

The one on the left illustrates a life with self in control, and depicts a stressful, chaotic life.

The circle on the right represents a life with Jesus Christ in control, balanced and orderly, with the potential for rich, productive experiences.

 Or

Which circle best represents you?

Objective: To evaluate your relationship with Christ

Read: John 4–6

Memorize: Galatians 6:7

Which circle would you like to have represent your life?

Meditate on each question in this lesson as well as on the answer. Make this a personal appraisal of your spiritual condition.

DO NOT BE DECIEUED
GOD CANNOT BE MOCKED A MAN REAPS WHAT HE SOWS

Bible Study

Types of Soil

Read the parable of the sower in Matthew 13:1–23; Mark 4:3–20; Luke 8:4–15.

1. To what does the seed refer (Mark 4:14)?

THE WORD OF GOD

2. What are the four kinds of soil referred to in Matthew 13:4–8?

1) *THE PATH*

2) *ROCKY*

3) *THORNS*

4) *GOOD SOIL*

Making Soil Productive

1. What does each kind of soil represent? Compare Matthew 13:4 with 18,19.

THE PATH REPRESENTS THE MISUNDERSTANDING OF THE GOSPEL MESSAGE AND OUR FAILURE TO RECOGNIZE IT.

Compare verses 5,6 with 20,21.

THE ROCKY SOIL REPRESENTS THE MAN WHO AT FIRST RECIEVES THE GOSPEL W/ JOY BUT DOES NOT MATURE + GROW W/ THE END RESULT BEING LOST AGAIN

Compare verse 7 with 22.

(MYSELF) THIS REPRESENTS THE MAN WHO HEARS AND RECIEVES THE WORD, BUT ULTIMATELY HIS PRIORITIES + WORRIES OF THIS WORLD STUNT HIS GROWTH, AND HE DOES NOT MATURE

Compare verse 8 with 23. *THE GOOD SOIL REPRESENTS THE MAN WHO RECIEVED THE WORD, ACTED ON IT AND PRODUCE A GOD CENTERED LIFE & TESTIMONY*

2. What must happen for the roadside soil to be changed (Hebrews 3:15)? *- IT MUST BE "TILLED" AND CULTIVATED" SO THE SEED WILL TAKE ROOT.*

3. How can unproductive, rocky ground be made productive (1 Corinthians 10:13 and Proverbs 29:25)? *By TRUSTING THE LORD, REMOVING THE "ROCKS" BY ACTING AND BELIEVING HIS WORD AS TRUE + INFALLIBLE*

4. How can individuals described as thorny soil become vital and effective Christians (1 Peter 5:7; Matthew 6:19–21)? *FIRST BY PUTTING THIS WORLD AND ITS WORRIES IN GOD'S HANDS, & KNOW HE IS IN CONTROL, AND BY STRIVING + WORKING TO DO THE FATHER'S WILL*

Result of Dwelling in Good Soil

1. What condition in a Christian results in abundance of fruit (Mark 4:20; Luke 8:15)? *THEY ACCEPT, RETAIN AND ACT ON THE WORD OF GOD.*

2. What type of soil do most of the professing Christians you know represent? *~ GOOD SOIL, ARE THE ONES I AM MOST DRAWN TO, BUT I'M TOUGH TO THINK WE ALL KNOW ONES IN ALL THE SOIL*

3. What type of soil would you say your life now represents? *GOOD SOIL, I ALSO KNOW THAT THE THORNS CAN SPRING UP UNEXPECTADLY SO I AM PREPARING MYSELF FOR THAT*

4. What type of soil do you want your life to represent? *GOOD SOIL, I LONG & SEEK IT JER 29:13*

LIFE APPLICATION

1 How must the soil of your life be changed to become good ground or to increase in its fruitfulness?

FIRST I ~~REC~~ NOW RECOGNIZE THAT MY LIFE IS NOT MY OWN BUT IT IS CHRIST WHO LIVES IN ME, AND THAT IN ORDER TO BEAR "FRUIT" I MUST BE OBEDIENT AND SUBMIT MYSELF TO HIS LEADING

2 List several problem areas that need changing.

ANGER, ENVY, SELFISNESS, MONEY DO YOU WANT TO KEEP GOING?

3 What must you trust Christ to do? TO TAKE CARE OF ALL OF MY NEEDS, TO CAST ALL MY ANXIETIES ON HIM BECAUSE HE CARES FOR ME
1 PES:7

❖ ❖ ❖

Living Abundantly

Imagine coming home one day to find a stain in your brand new living room carpet. You try everything possible to take out the discoloration. Nothing seems to work. Then someone gives you a special formula guaranteed to remove even the worst of stains. The spot remover is so powerful that it not only takes out the blotch, but it also protects the carpet from ever being blemished again.

This is what God does with our sins. Christ's excruciating death on the cross forever blotted out our unrighteousness. No sin is too deep, no stain too dark, that God cannot cleanse us to a brilliant white through the precious blood of Jesus Christ.

Christ's sacrifice for us on the cross is complete. He saved us from the penalty of sin (John 3:18; Ephesians 2:8). We are being saved from the power of sin (Jude 24,25; 2 Thessalonians 3:3). And we will be saved from the presence of sin (1 John 3:2; Philippians 3:21; 1 Corinthians 15:51,52).

You have trusted God for the payment of your penalty for sin and for eternal life. Why not trust Him now for power over sin? Remember that as you received Christ by faith, so you should walk in faith and receive the abundant life that He has promised you.

❖

Objective: To learn the steps to abundant life

Read: John 7–9

Memorize: John 10:10

THE THIEF COMES ONLY TO STEAL AND KILL AND DESTROY
I HAVE COME THAT THEY MAY HAVE LIFE AND HAVE IT
TO THE FULL

31

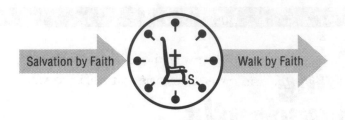

Bible Study

The Basis of Abundant Living
Read Romans 6:1–23.

1. What do you know happened to you when you became a Christian (verse 6)? *SIN IN US DIED, THAT IS WE ARE NO LONGER CONTROLLED BY IT, BUT HAVE BEEN SET FREE.*

2. According to verse 11, what must you do? *DEAD TO SIN, ALIVE TO GOD, (LIVE FOR CHRIST)*

3. According to verse 13, what is your responsibility? *TO OFFER OUR LIVES TO CHRIST AND RIGHTEOUSNESS NOT TO SIN & DESTRUCTION*

4. According to verse 16, man is a servant either of sin or of righteousness. What determines his allegiance? *THE ONE WHO YOU OBEY*

Review Romans 6:6,11,13,16 and note the progression:
◆ *Know* that you have been crucified with Christ.
◆ *Count* yourself dead to sin and alive to Jesus Christ.

◆ *Offer* yourself unto God.

◆ *Obey* God.

(See Directory of Terms on the following page.)

Using these four steps, dedicate yourself to serving God rather than sin.

5. Describe the benefits you have already seen from righteous living. *THE GOD HAS CLEANSED ME & WASHED ME CLEAN BY THE BLOOD OF CHRIST, THAT AS I WALK WITH CHRIST MY PATHS ARE DIRECTED BY HIM, MY LIFE IS HIS & NOT MY OWN.*

The Practice of Abundant Living

Read Psalm 37:1–7,34.

1. What wrong attitudes are given in verse 1?

ENVY, WORRYING

2. What is to be your attitude toward the Lord (verse 3)?

TRUST HIM, DELIGHT IN HIM, COMMIT MY LIFE TO HIM

3. What must you do to receive the desires of your heart (verse 4)? *MAKE THE LORD KING OF MY LIFE & REJOICE IN HIS PRESENCE & WORKING IN MY LIFE*

4. Why is it necessary to consider verse 5 when you plan your future? *God knows beginning and end and what is best for us BECAUSE WHEN WE GIVE OUR LIFES TO THE LORD OUR ATTITUDES AND DESIRES ARE TO SERVE HIM AND HIS WILL FOR OUR LIVES*

5. How can you apply the instruction in verse 7? Be specific. *FIRST TO KEEP MY EYES AND ATTENTION ON THE LORD, TO COMMIT ALL OUR WAYS TO HIM, IN EVERYTHING WE DO GLORIFY HIM, DON'T LOOK AT WORLDLY THINGS AND THE MEN WHO POSSESS THESE THINGS, KEEP OUR FOCUS ON JESUS CHRIST*

6. What does verse 34 mean to you? *BE PATIENT, GOD'S TIMING IS NOT OUR TIMING, WE WILL ONE DAY BE HELD HIGH ABOVE, WHEN THE JUDGEMENT IS NEAR, THE WICKED WILL PERISH, AND WE WILL BE LIFTED UP.*

Now, review each of the above references and note the progression:

◆ Do not *fret*.

◆ *Trust* in the Lord.

◆ *Delight* yourself in the Lord.

◆ *Commit* your way to the Lord.

◆ *Be still* before the Lord.

◆ *Wait* on the Lord.

(See Directory of Terms below.)

The secret of the abundant life is contained in these key words: *know, count, offer, obey, fret not, trust, delight, commit, be still,* and *wait.* (Underline these words in Romans 6 and Psalm 37 in your Bible.)

Directory of Terms

Know—to be fully assured of a fact

Count—to act upon a fact, to consider it, to depend upon it instead of upon feelings

Offer—to give up, to surrender, to submit

Obey—to put instructions into effect, to comply with, to trust

Fret not—to give up worry and anxiety

Trust—to rely on wholeheartedly

Delight—to take great pleasure or joy

Commit—to place in trust or charge, to entrust

Be still—to completely listen

Wait—to anticipate with confident expectancy

LIFE APPLICATION

1 In the chart below, indicate which key words of the abundant life you are now applying, and which you need to begin to apply, through the power of Christ.

KEY WORDS	APPLYING NOW (✓)	NEED TO APPLY (✓)
KNOW	✓	
COUNT	✓	
OFFER		✓
OBEY	✓	
FRET NOT		✓
TRUST	✓	
DELIGHT	✓	
COMMIT	✓	
BE STILL		✓
WAIT	✓	

2 How do you plan to apply these? Be specific.

I FIND MYSELF SOMETIMES THINKING EMOTIONALLY & WORRYING, INSTEAD OF ACTING ON THE WORD OF GOD, ALSO I AM REALIZING I AM GETTING AHEAD OF GOD.

❖ ❖ ❖

The Abiding Life

Alex was distressed over his constant failure to live the Christian life victoriously.

"I'm always failing," he said. "I know what is right, but I'm simply not able to keep the many commitments, resolutions, and rededications that I make to the Lord almost daily.

"What's wrong with me? Why do I constantly fail? How can I push that magic button that will change my life and make me the kind of person God wants me to be, and the kind of person I want to be?"

All of us experience this conflict when we walk in our own strength. But the victory is ours as we learn to abide in Christ.

Jesus said, "I am the vine, you are the branches. He who abides in Me, and I in him, bears much fruit; for without Me you can do nothing" (John 15:5, NKJ). The reality of abiding in Christ and Christ abiding in us is made possible through a supernatural enabling of the Holy Spirit.

Abiding in Christ means to be one with Him by faith. It is to live in conscious dependence upon Him, recognizing that it is His life, His power, His wisdom, His strength, and His ability operating through us that enable us to live according to His will. We do this by

❖

Objective: To understand and begin abiding in Christ

Read: John 10–12

Memorize: John 15:7,16

37

surrendering the throne of our lives to Him, and by faith drawing upon His resources to live a supernatural, holy fruitful life.

The "abiding life"—we in Christ, He in us—enables us to live a victorious and fruitful life. Millions of Christians throughout the world profess their love for Christ each week by attending church services, singing songs, studying their Bibles, and attending prayer meetings. Yet, all the talk in the world will never convince anyone that you or I truly love the Lord unless we obey Him, and this includes bearing fruit for Him. The only way we can demonstrate that we are truly abiding in Him is to produce fruit, which involves introducing others to our Savior as well as living holy lives.

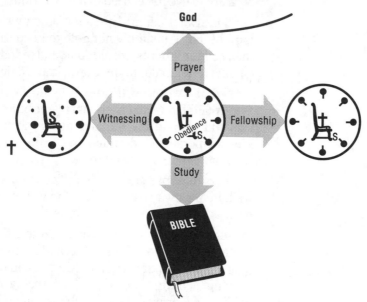

The "abiding life" also brings lasting joy. "I have told you this," Jesus said, "so that my joy may be in you and that your joy may be complete."

To live this joyful, abundant life, we must learn to live in Christ, constantly yielding total control of our lives to Him.

Is the abiding presence of Jesus Christ a reality in your life? As an expression of your will, in prayer, surrender the throne of your life to Him, and by faith invite Him to endow you with supernatural life and enable you to bear much fruit for His glory.

❖
Bible Study

The Abiding Life

"Abiding is the key to Christian experience by which the divine attributes are transplanted into human soil, to the transforming of character and conduct."

—Norman B. Harrison

1. In John 15:5, Jesus referred to Himself as the ___VINE___ and Christians as the ___BRANCHES___.

What is the relationship between Christ and you, as illustrated in that verse? *THAT THE BRANCHES CANNOT LIVE AND BEAR FRUIT WITHOUT THE VINE, THAT IS I CANNOT LIVE A "FRUITFUL" CHRISTIAN LIFE WITHOUT CHRIST AS THE "VINE".*

2. Why does Jesus prune every branch that bears fruit (John 15:2)? *SO THAT WE WILL EVEN BE MORE "FRUITFUL".*

What are some experiences you can identify as "pruning" in your life as a Christian? (See Hebrews 12:6; Romans 5:3–5.)

SINCE 1993 WHEN I ASK JESUS INTO MY LIFE, I HAVE ASKED FOR GUIDANCE AND "PRUNING". I KNOW MY INTENTIONS WERE NOT TO GLORIFY GOD BUT WERE SELF-CENTERED, I THINK THE LAST 3 MONTHS HAVE BEEN GOD'S REFINING & PRUNING

What were the results?

AS A RESULT I HAVE COME TO REALIZE MY FOCUS IS AND SHOULD BE GOD CENTERED, DON SHONE IS DEAD, I BELONG TO CHRIST AND I STRIVE TO RUN THE RACE HE HAS MARKED OUT FOR ME, TO PUT WORLDLY DESIRES BEHIND, AND GIVE GOD EVERYTHING. Good Praise God

What did you learn through these situations?

I HAVE LEARNED THAT GOD IS FAITHFUL, FORGIVING AND JUST. HE DISCIPLINES US BECAUSE HE LOVES US AND ALSO THAT I WILL STRIVE TO GIVE HIM ALL MY CONCERNS AND DISAPPOINTMENTS. God is faithful He won't let you down!

Results of Abiding in Christ

1. Read John 15:7–11.

   List two necessary qualifications for effective prayer according to verse 7.

   1) *REMAIN CHRIST*

   2) *REMAIN IN THE WORD*

2. Jesus glorified God. How can you glorify God (verse 8)?

   By DOING THE FATHER'S WILL, THUS SHOWING OURSELVES AS CHILDREN OF GOD.

3. Christ commands us to continue in His love. How great do you believe this love to be (verse 9)? *THIS LOVE IS IMMEASURABLE IN MY EYES.*

   How are we to abide in Christ's love (verse 10)?

   By OBEYING HIS COMMANDS, AND DOING HIS WILL.

   How do you think the result promised in verse 11 will be revealed in your life today? *— TO SEE GOD WORKING SO INTIMATELY IN NOT ONLY MY LIFE, (WITNESSING OPPURTUNITIES, PRAYER) BUT WORKING THROUGHOUT THIS CELLBLOCK, IN THE FORM OF SO MANY ANSWERED PRAYERS, FOR MEN WHO ARE UNSAVED, GOD CONSTANTLY IS MAKING HIMSELF KNOWN.*

4. What has Christ chosen us to do (John 15:16)?

TO GO AND BEAR FRUIT, TO LIVE AS CHRIST LIVED, IN HUMBLENESS, + MEEKNESS SO THAT OUR LOVE MAY BE EVIDENT TO ALL

What is meant by "fruit"? (See Matthew 4:19; Galatians 5:22,23; Ephesians 5:9; Philippians 1:11.) *EVANGELISM,*

FRUITS OF THE SPIRIT, LOVE, JOY PEACE, PATIENCE KINDNESS, GOODNESS, FAITHFULNESS, GENTLENESS, SELF CONTROL, TRUTH, RIGHTEOUSNESS A godly life and the souls of men and women.

5. Why do you think Jesus chose this particular way to illustrate our abiding in Him? *BECAUSE OF THE WICKEDNESS OF THIS WORLD, WHATEVER IS CONTRARY TO THAT STANDS OUT, THAT IS WE ARE SHINING LIGHTS BUT ALSO BECAUSE GOD IS LOVE, AND THERE IS NO LAW FOR LOVE*

6. Will you be able to do what Christ expects of you?

ONLY THROUGH THE STRENGTH OF THE HOLY SPIRIT, BECAUSE I CAN DO ALL THINGS THROUGH HIM THAT STRENGTHENS ME

How do you know?

GOD'S WORD TELLS ME THAT, I BELIEVE IT AND WILL ACT ON IT. I'VE LEARNED TO LEAN NOT ON MY OWN UNDERSTANDING, THAT THIS BATTLE HAS ALREADY BEEN WON AND I REST IN THE INFALLIBLE WORD OF GOD.

LIFE APPLICATION

1 Write briefly what you need to do to begin abiding in
Christ more consistently. I NEED AND LONG
FOR HUMILITY + MEEKNESS, TO SEEK HIM
IN ALL CIRCUMSTANCES, TO PUT CHRIST
AT THE CENTER OF MY LIFE AND ALWAYS
REMEMBER THAT MY LIFE IS NOT MY OWN
ANY LONGER

2 What do you think He will do as a result?
GIVE ME THE DESIRES OF MY HEART
ACCORDING TO HIS WILL, GIVE ME PEACE
WHICH TRANSCENDS ALL UNDERSTANDING,
AND MOST IMPORTANTLY HE WILL ABIDE IN
ME

3 How do you think that will affect your life?
THE THINGS THAT HAVE BEEN DEFECTIVE
IN MY LIFE WILL BE REMOVED, I WILL
BECOME (AS I MATURE) PURE AND BLAMELESS
CHILDREN OF GOD AS I HOLD OUT THE
WORDS OF LIFE,
        THANK YOU JESUS!

❖   ❖   ❖

The Cleansed Life

If the Holy Spirit was sent to give me power to live a victorious life, why do I feel so powerless, so defeated?

We often yearn for spiritual power and do not have it because of impure motives, selfish desires, or unconfessed sin. God does not fill a dirty vessel with His power and love. The vessel of our lives must be cleansed by the blood of our Lord before it can be filled with the Spirit of God.

The psalmist wrote, "Search me, O God, and know my heart; test me and know my anxious thoughts. See if there is any offensive way in me, and lead me in the way everlasting" (Psalm 139:23,24).

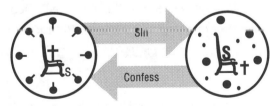

❖

Objective: To learn the importance and means of living a cleansed life, moment by moment

Read: John 13–15

Memorize: 1 John 1:9

I believe that this prayer is an essential discipline of the Christian's inner life. It expresses to God our desire for purity, our longing to make His ways our ways. Asking Him to reveal to us any unconfessed sin enables us to keep our accounts short with

IF WE CONFESS OUR SINS HE IS FAITHFULL AND JUST AND WILL FORGIVE US OUR SINS AND CLEANSE US FROM ALL UNRIGTEOUSNESS

Him. Confession results in cleansing. God's Word promises, "If we confess our sins, he is faithful and just and will forgive us our sins and purify us from all unrighteousness (1 John 1:9).

The Holy Spirit longs to fill us with His power and love. In this lesson, you will learn how your life can have this power. The first step is to be cleansed from sin and filled with the Spirit of God.

Bible Study

Living "Out of Fellowship" With God
Study the preceding diagram.

1. What characterizes a person who is not in fellowship with God (James 1:8)? HE IS DOUBLEMINDED, UNSTABLE, THAT IS HE DOES NOT PUT THE THINGS OF GOD FIRST

Think back on your life. How has this verse characterized you? – FROM EARLY FEB TO MAY I DEFINETELY WAS THIS WAY, SINCE I WAS NO LONGER IGNORANT OF GOD'S WAYS I WAS CARNAL AND ENTRENCHED IN SIN

In what way(s) has this changed since you came to know Jesus Christ? – I NOW AM BEING GIVEN OPPURTUNITIES TO GIVE EVERYTHING TO HIM. I KNOW WHEN I AM RELEASED I START WITH A CLEAN SLATE

2. Read Isaiah 59:2. What is the result of sin in one's life? THAT OUR COMMUNICATION WITH GOD IS BLOCKED, GOD CANNOT DWELL IN SIN, SO IN TURN UNCONFESSED SIN KEEPS GOD FROM HEARING OUR PRAYERS

3. Do you think sin in your life has affected your relationship with God? How? *YES, IT HAS STAGNATED MY SPIRITUAL GROWTH, HINDERED BLESSINGS, BROKEN FELLOWSHIP, AND GRIEVED GOD.*

How to be Cleansed

1. What is the condition for cleansing and forgiveness (1 John 1:9)? *– WE MUST CONFESS OUR SIN TO GOD + HE WILL WIPE OUR SLATE CLEAN, + THROUGH FAITHFULNESS, + JUSTIFICATION*

The word confess means "to say the same thing as another—to agree with God."

Confession involves three things:

◆ Agreeing that you have sinned (be specific)

◆ Agreeing that Christ's death on the cross paid the penalty for that sin

◆ Repentance—changing your attitude toward that sin, which will result in a change of action toward that sin

When God brings to your attention the fact that something you have done is sin, you are to confess—say the same thing God says about that specific sin. Do not just say, "I have sinned," but state what the sin was and agree with God, looking at it from His viewpoint. Then determine to put it out of your life and not do it again.

2. What two things did the psalmist do about his sin in Psalm 32:5?

1) *ACKNOWLEDGED IT*

2) *CONFESS IT*

Read Proverbs 28:13. What is the result of not admitting sin?

WE DO NOT PROSPER IN THE BLESSINGS OF GOD

Of admitting sin? WE FIND MERCY

3. In what situations has each of these results been true in your life? – RECENT MORAL DEFICITNCY, FOLLOWED BY BEING DISCIPLINED WHICH LED TO TRUE REPENTANCE

Living "In Fellowship" With God

1. Notice in the diagram on page 43 that, when we confess our sins, God restores us to fellowship. Walking in fellowship with the Father and the Son is referred to as "walking in the light."

   Read 1 John 1:7 and list two results promised.

   1) WE HAVE FELLOWSHIP

   2) PURIFY'S US FROM SIN

   Give an example of how you have experienced each in your life. MY RENEWED WALK WITH THE LORD KNOWING I HAVE BEEN FORGIVEN, NOT DWELLING ON IT, BUT MOVING FORWARD WITH MY WALK 😊

2. When we are in fellowship with God, specific things are happening within us. According to Philippians 2:13 and 4:13, what are they? WE ACT + WALK WITH GODLY PERSPECTIVE, KNOWING WE CAN DO ALL THINGS THROUGH HIM WHO GIVES US STRENGTH

Describe how the verses can help you overcome specific temptations or weaknesses you face. WHEN I NEED TO DEAL WITH ANGER, I WILL GIVE IT TO THE LORD, SEEK FELLOWSHIP AND PRAYER AND ACTING ON THE WORD OF GOD.

3. What is this power within us and what is its result (Romans 8:9; Galatians 5:22,23)? HOLY SPIRIT THE FRUITS OF THE SPIRIT, LOVE, JOY, PEACE PATIENCE, KINDNESS, GOODNESS, FAITHFULNESS, GENTLENESS AND SELF CONTROL

List several ways the qualities found in Galatians 5:22,23 are at work in your life. — THEY HELP ME DEALING WITH THE MEN HERE WHO ARE UNBELIEVERS SO THAT I CAN BE A LIVING TESTIMONY FOR JESUS CHRIST IN ALL I SAY, DO.

4. What should be our attitude when tempted (Romans 6:11–14)? DEAD TO SIN, DO NOT LET SIN HAVE CONTROLE OVER YOUR BODIES, OR OFFER YOUR BODIES TO SIN BUT OFFER YOUR BODIES AS LIVING

Why (Colossians 3:3)? SACRIFICES TO BECAUSE I DIED TO SIN AND MY LIFE IS NOW HIDDEN w/ CHRIST JESUS

Identify ways you can obey the instructions given in Romans 6:11–14. — SELF-CONTROL, PRAYER, ACCOUNTABILITY, FELLOWSHIP, ACTING ON GOD'S WORD THROUGH FAITH

LIFE APPLICATION

1 In your own words, write what you will do when you find anything that breaks your fellowship with the Lord.

FIRST I WILL CONFESS IT AS SUCH, ASKING GOD TO GIVE ME THE DETERMINATION AND STRENGTH TO TURN FROM IT, REPENT AND KNOW JESUS PAID THE PRICE FOR MY SIN

2 Summarize the reasons it is so important to confess sin as soon as you are aware of it. SO THAT FELLOWSHIP WITH GOD IS UNHINDERED, AND THAT THE BLESSINGS OF GOD CAN BE POURED OUT ON US.

3 Use these steps to confess your sin:
   1) Ask the Holy Spirit to reveal the sins in your life.
   2) List the sins on a piece of paper.
   3) Confess the sins.
   4) Write 1 John 1:9 across the sins.
   5) Thank God for His complete forgiveness.
   6) Destroy the paper to signify what happened to your sins.

❖   ❖   ❖

Victorious in Spiritual Warfare

Picture with me for a moment a British soldier in the Revolutionary War. Along with his fellow soldiers, he fought against the Colonial forces, who were brilliantly led by General George Washington. As the small Colonial army fought against the overwhelming, superior troops of England, they were miraculously victorious. Even so, there were several British soldiers who refused to surrender. They refused to admit their defeat, and they continued with guerrilla activity.

This is the portrait of the Christian life. We read in Colossians 1:13,14 that God has rescued us out of the darkness and gloom of Satan's kingdom. The Christian flag of victory has been raised; Satan has been defeated. Yet the spiritual guerrilla warfare continues.

If we are to walk in the control and fullness of the Holy Spirit, we must be prepared for spiritual conflict.

I am sure there are dozens of times every day—at home, at the office, at the grocery store, while driving on the freeway—that you face temptations to compromise your Christian convictions. None of us in this life have gotten to the point of perfection. I can tell you

❖

Objective: To learn of spiritual warfare and how to use the things God has provided for the battle

Read: John 16–18

Memorize: Ephesians 6:10–12

FINALLY, BE STRONG IN THE LORD AND IN HIS MIGHTY POWER. PUT ON THE FULL ARMOR OF GOD SO THAT YOU CAN TAKE YOUR STAND AGAINST THE DEVIL'S SCHEMES. FOR OUR STRUGGLE IS NOT AGAINST FLESH AND BLOOD BUT AGAINST THE RULERS, AGAINST THE AUTHORITIES, AGAINST

49

that even after almost fifty years of walking with our wonderful Lord, I face such guerrilla warfare daily.

Ephesians 6:10–18 exhorts us to "put on all of God's armor so that you will be able to stand safe against all the strategies and tricks of Satan."

There are ways you can deal with the "guerrillas" in your life. Let me list just a few:

1. *Confess all known sin in your life.* Sin is the result of disobedience, and it gives Satan a stronghold in our lives.

2. *Center your affections on Christ and surrender to His Lordship.* The apostle Paul records in Romans 12:2, "Don't copy the behavior and customs of this world, but be a new and different person with a fresh newness in all you do and think" (TLB).

3. *Know that as an act of your will by faith, you can be free in Christ.* Romans 6:16 says: "Don't you realize that you can choose your own master? You can choose sin [with death] or else obedience [with acquittal]" (TLB).

4. *Be filled with the Spirit.* You are filled with the Spirit in the same way you became a Christian—by faith (Ephesians 5:18).

5. *Study God's holy, inspired Word daily.* Prayerfully apply its truths to your life.

6. *Experience daily the power of prayer.* As a child of God you are invited to come boldly before His throne to receive His mercy and find grace in your time of need (Hebrews 4:14–16).

7. *Live by faith.* Everything you receive from God, from the moment of your spiritual birth until you die, is by faith. It is impossible to please God without faith (Hebrews 11:6).

Christ died to win the victory over all the guerrillas in our lives. I encourage you to begin applying these principles to your life today, and He will help you to be strong in Him.

Bible Study

Describe in your own words the picture
depicted in Paul's command given
in Ephesians 6:10–18.

Helmet of Salvation

Breast Plate of Righteousness

Belt of Truth

Shield of Faith

Sword of the Spirit (Word of God)

Shoes to Spread the Gospel of Peace

TO PROTECT YOUR HEART,
MIND, THROUGH RIGHTEOUSNESS,
USING THE SHIELD OF FAITH,
THE WORD OF GOD, +
THE SPREADING OF THE
GOSPEL TO OVERCOME +
DESTROY ALL OF SATAN'S
SCHEMES

We Are On the Battlefield

1. What two things will putting on the whole armor of God
   help you to do (verses 10,11)?

   1) STRONG IN THE LORD

   2) STAND AGAINST SATAN'S SCHEMES

   How are we to defend ourselves against our enemies
   (verses 10–13)? - THROUG TAKING A STAND, BE FIRM
   IN YOUR FAITH, USING GOD'S WORD, YOUR FAITH, AND BY
   DOING THE WILL OF GOD (SPREADING THE GOSPEL) putting on
                                                the armor of God.

2. Who are the enemies?

   James 4:4 THE WORLD AND ALL WHO ARE OF
   THE WORLD.

Galatians 5:16,17

THE SINFUL NATURE THAT IS IN US
THE SINFUL DESIRES OF OUR HEARTS

(1 Peter 5:8) *BE SELF CONTROLLED AND ALERT*

Who are our enemies?
↓ *Devil*

3. Name the six protective pieces of armor that God provides
and expects you to wear (Ephesians 6:14–17).

1) *HELMET OF SALVATION (MIND)*

2) *BREASTPLATE OF RIGHTEOUSNESS (HEART)*

3) *BELT OF TRUTH (RI HONESTY)*

4) *SHIELD OF FAITH*

5) *SWORD OF THE SPIRIT (PRAYER)*

6) *SHOES OF EAGERNESS TO SPREAD THE GOSPEL*
Gospel of Peace

4. How can you employ the sword of God's Word (verse 17)
for defense against temptation (Psalm 119:9,11)?
LIVE + ACT ON THE WORD OF GOD PLANTING ON
OUR HEARTS,

5. List some ways the sword of God's Word can be used in an
offensive action (2 Timothy 3:16,17). *BY TEACHING, REBUKING,*
CORRECTING, AND TRAINING IN GOD'S WAYS. SO
THAT WE CAN BE PREPARED AND ACT ON GOD'S WORD.

6. How can you stay alert and always be prepared
(Ephesians 6:18; Colossians 4:2)? *THROUGH PRAYER NOT*
ONLY FOR YOURSELF BUT FOR ALL THE BROTHERS,
BUT ALSO TO BE ON GUARD, AND THANK GOD
FOR ANSWERING PRAYERS

We Are More Than Conquerors Through Christ!

1. How should you respond to these enemies?

Romans 12:2 - *By NOT CONFORMING TO THE WORLD AND RENEWING YOUR MIND BY THE WORD OF GOD, THEN YOU WILL BE ABLE TO KNOW GOD'S WILL IN YOUR LIFE HIS PERFECT WILL*

Galatians 5:16 *BY LIVING BY THE SPIRIT, DOING WHAT GOD'S WILL HIS.*

James 4:7 *By SUBMITTING TO GOD, DRAW NEAR TO HIM AND HE WILL DRAW NEAR TO YOU*

2. When you consider the pieces of armor and weapons provided, who can you conclude is really fighting the battle (Ephesians 6:10)? *THE LORD JESUS CHRIST*

3. Why can you always expect God to be the winner (1 John 4:4)? *BECAUSE I AM A CHILD OF GOD. and the one who is in you is greater than He who is in the world.*

4. How does Romans 8:31 affect your attitude toward adversity and temptation? *BECAUSE GOD IS FOR US NOBODY CAN BE AGAINST US.*

5. How do these principles help you to live a more abundant life? *I KNOW THAT GOD HAS GIVEN ME THE VICTORY AT CALVARY, NOW I KNOW I NEED TO ACT + WALK IN THE VICTORY*

LIFE APPLICATION

1 Describe a specific situation in your life right now in which you need to employ a spiritual "weapon."

JUST TODAY (7/27) I WAS ACCUSED BY THE
JUDGE OF BEING DISHONEST, I DID NOT
REACT, BUT ACTED ON THE WORD OF GOD, KNOWING
WHAT I SAID TO BE THE TRUTH. GOD WILL
JUSTIFY ME AND SUSTAIN ME ACCORDING TO
HIS WILL (HELMET OF SALVATION)

2 Which weapon(s) will you use and how?

I WILL ALSO USE THE SHIELD OF FAITH,
AND THE SWORD OF THE SPIRIT OF
PRAYER.

3 What results do you expect? THAT GOD WILL
GIVE ME A PEACE THAT TRANSCENDS ALL
UNDERSTANDING, WALKING, AND ACTING IN
FAITH, KNOWING HE IS IN CONTROL

❖   ❖   ❖

Attitude Makes the Difference

Your son has just been rushed into the emergency room at the hospital. He was severely injured in a traffic accident, and is not expected to live…

You've just discovered that your teenage daughter is pregnant…

The house payment is past due; the dentist is threatening to turn your bill over to collection. Your telephone has been shut off, and you're facing a layoff at the plant…

Your husband is a hopeless alcoholic. He becomes violent when he is drunk…

Crisis is part of life. We cannot escape difficulty. Jesus said, "In this world you will have trouble" (John 16:33). In short, life is a battleground. But it is not the crisis that creates the problem; it is how we react to it. The pain of trouble can be eased by the attitude we take toward it.

When two Christians face the same tragedy, one may become depressed and defeated while the other draws closer to God. What do you think is the reason for this?

❖

Objective: To begin looking at life consistently from God's perspective

Read: John 19–21

Memorize: 2 Corinthians 1:3,4

PRAISE BE TO GOD AND FATHER OF OUR LORD JESUS CHRIST, THE FATHER OF COMPASSION AND THE GOD OF ALL COMFORT, WHO COMFORTS US IN ALL OUR TROUBLES, SO THAT WE CAN COMFORT THOSE IN ANY TROUBLE WITH THE COMFORT WE OURSELVES HAVE RECIEVED FROM GOD

55

Sometimes Christians believe that God has let them down when they find themselves without money, health, or prestige, or in severe straits. Such an attitude leads to coldness of heart, prayerlessness, distrust, worry, and selfish living.

In this study you will learn about unrecognized blessings and how attitude makes the difference between a defeated outlook and a victorious one.

❖

Bible Study

God's People in Trouble

In Exodus 14:1–4, the Israelites experienced an unrecognized blessing. As you read, notice the human viewpoint of the people and God's viewpoint as seen in Moses.

1. How did the Israelites react to apparent danger (Exodus 14:10–12)? *THEY WERE TERRIFIED*

2. Notice how Moses reacted. Why do you think he commanded the people as he did (Exodus 14:13,14)?
BECAUSE MOSES ACTED ON FAITH AND THE WORD OF GOD

3. What did God accomplish in their hearts and minds through this experience (Exodus 14:31)? *THE ISRAELITES THEN TRUSTED AND FEARED (REVERED) THE LORD*

4. Think back to a crisis in your life. How did those around
you respond? *SOME IN PITY, SOME IN DISGUST SOME IN DISAPPOINTMENT*

How did you react?
WITH REPENTENCE WITH ANGER, WITH DISAPPOINTMENT, WITH A PITY PARTY

How could you have improved your attitude? *I EVENTUALLY REPENTED, WAS FORGIVEN AND I NOW LOOK FORWARD TO THE MINISTRY JOURNEY GOD HAS FOR ME.*

List ways God has worked through difficulties in your life,
and has shown these difficulties really to be blessings.

BY MY BEING ARRESTED I WAS RESCUED! DELIVERED FROM DRUGS AND ALCOHOL, LESS AM BEING RENEWED DAILY, HAVE BEEN GIVEN MANY WITNESSING OPPORTUNITIES AND HAVE BEEN USED BY GOD TO BRING SOME MEN TO THE SAVING GRACE OF JESUS CHRIST

Taking the Proper Attitude

1. List some things the Bible guarantees when you are
tempted or tested (1 Corinthians 10:13). *WE WILL NOT BE TEMPTED BEYOND WHAT WE CAN BEAR, AND THAT GOD WILL PROVIDE A WAY OUT.*

2. How can the Bible's guarantee in Romans 8:28 be true that
everything will work out for good to those who love God?

BY TRUSTING GOD, AND ACTING ON HIS WORD

When have you ever doubted God's work in your life? Why?
WHEN I FIRST ENTERED COOK COUNTY JAIL TO SHARE MY
TESTIMONY IN JUNE OF 96' - FEAR OF GOING BACK TO JAIL,
FEAR OF REJECTION, BEING UNSURE.

3. What response to tribulation does God expect from you,
according to Romans 5:3–5? TO REJOICE KNOWING THAT
IT BUILDS OUR PERSEVERANCE, CHARACTER, HOPE, KNOWING
THAT GOD IS POURING HIS LOVE OUT ON US.

What are the results of tribulations? (See also James 1:3.)
IT BUILDS OUR FAITH AND DEVELOPS
PERSEVERANCE.

4. What is the purpose of unrecognized blessings according to:
2 Corinthians 1:3,4 - THAT WE WILL RECOGNIZE AND
ACKNOWLEDGE GOD'S COMPASSION TO US SO THAT
WE CAN IN TURN COMFORT THOSE WHO NEED COMFORTING

Hebrews 12:5–11 THAT WE RECOGNIZE GOD'S
GOD'S DISCIPLINE AS HIS SHOW OF LOVE TO US, AND
ENDURE HARDSHIP, SO WE OBEY GOD'S WORD

5. Read 1 Thessalonians 5:18 and Hebrews 13:15.
What response does God command in *all* situations?
GIVE THANKS IN ALL CIRCUMSTANCES

How can you rejoice and give thanks when sorrow and
tragedy come? — BY OUR UNWAVERING FAITH
AND ACTING ON THE WORD OF GOD, KNOWING
ALL THINGS WORK FOR GOOD FOR THOSE WHO LOVE THE
                                                              LORD
Contrast this with the attitude of the Israelites in   DISCIPLINE
Exodus 14:1–12. THEY DID NOT SEE THE ~~BLESSINGS~~
AS ~~DISCIPLINE~~ BLESSINGS BUT AS PERSECUTION AND PUNISHMENT
THEY ALSO FAILED TO REJOICE IN GOD'S BUILDING
OF THEIR FAITH.

LIFE APPLICATION

1 List the methods by which an attitude of trust can become a reality for you. (See Ephesians 5:18; Galatians 5:16; 1 Thessalonians 5:17; Romans 10:17.)

LIVING BY THE SPIRIT, PRAY CONTINUALLY BY LIVING, HEARING, READING AND ACTING ON THE WORD OF GOD.

2 With what trial in your life do you need to trust God right now? *FOR MY FUTURE, IT'S JUST SO HARD TO FATHOM.*

3 What do you think the unrecognized blessings in that trial could be? *- JER 29:11-13 KNOWING GOD HAS A PLAN FOR ME.*

4 How can you receive those blessings? *- BELIEVING AND TRUSTING GOD. BY LIVING DAY BY DAY IN GOD'S WORD, BE LEAD BY THE SPIRIT IN ALL I DO, RECOGNIZING AND ADMITTING THAT MY LIFE IS NOT MY OWN BUT I LIVE FOR CHRIST.*

❖ ❖ ❖

You did not do "Recap" on next page. Look at the questions. Think about them. We are praying for you. God is with you.

Recap

The following questions will help you review this Step. If necessary, reread the appropriate lesson(s).

1. In your own words, what does the abundant Christian life involve?

2. Envision and describe the abundant life you desire for yourself.

What part does bearing fruit have?

What part does spiritual warfare play?

Reread: Luke 8:4–5; Romans 6:1–16; John 15:1–17; 1 John 1:1–9

Review: Verses memorized

3. How do you know your picture of the abundant life is consistent with God's view?

LIFE APPLICATION

1 What specific steps do you still need to take to make the abundant life a reality for you?

2 List verses from Lesson 6 that can help you deal with temptations you face. Each week, update this list to include additional temptations and the verses to help you deal with them.

TEMPTATION	VERSE

Resources to Help You Live Abundantly

Life Without Equal. A presentation of the length and breadth of the Christian's freedom in Jesus Christ and how believers can release Christ's resurrection power for life and ministry. Good for unbelievers or Christians who want to grow in their Christian life.

Ten Basic Steps. A comprehensive curriculum for the Christian who wants to master the basics of Christian growth. Used by hundreds of thousands worldwide. (See page 63 for details.)

The Ten Basic Steps Leader's Guide. Contains Bible study outlines for teaching the complete series.

A Handbook for Christian Maturity. Combines the entire series of the *Ten Basic Steps* in one volume. A handy resource for private Bible study, an excellent book to help nurture spiritual growth and maturity.

Five Steps of Christian Growth. Teaches new believers the five cornerstones of faith: assurance of salvation, understanding God's love, experiencing God's forgiveness, being filled with the Holy Spirit, and steps to growing in Christ.

Transferable Concept: How You Can Experience God's Love and Forgiveness. Illustrates that God has an exciting and victorious plan for those who accept His forgiveness from sin and obey His command to be controlled daily, moment-by-moment, by the Holy Spirit.

Keys to Dynamic Living card. Experience a joyful, fruitful, Spirit-filled life and deal with temptation through "spiritual breathing." Small enough to tuck into your pocket, purse, or Bible.

Ten Basic Steps Toward Christian Maturity

Eleven easy-to-use individual guides to help you understand the basics of the Christian faith

INTRODUCTION: The Uniqueness of Jesus

Explains who Jesus Christ is. Reveals the secret of His power to turn you into a victorious, fruitful Christian.

STEP 1: The Christian Adventure

Shows you how to enjoy a full, abundant, purposeful, and fruitful life in Christ.

STEP 2: The Christian and the Abundant Life

Explores the Christian way of life—what it is and how it works practically.

STEP 3: The Christian and the Holy Spirit

Teaches who the Holy Spirit is, how to be filled with the Spirit, and how to make the Spirit-filled life a moment-by-moment reality in your life.

STEP 4: The Christian and Prayer

Reveals the true purpose of prayer and shows how the Father, Son, and Holy Spirit work together to answer your prayers.

STEP 5: The Christian and the Bible

Talks about the Bible—how we got it, its authority, and its power to help the believer. Offers methods for studying the Bible more effectively.

STEP 6: The Christian and Obedience

Learn why it is so important to obey God and how to live daily in His grace. Discover the secret to personal purity and power as a Christian and why you need not fear what others think of you.

STEP 7: The Christian and Witnessing

Shows you how to witness effectively. Includes a reproduction of the *Four Spiritual Laws* and explains how to share them.

STEP 8: The Christian and Giving

Discover God's plan for your financial life, how to stop worrying about money, and how to trust God for your finances.

STEP 9: Exploring the Old Testament

Features a brief survey of the Old Testament. Shows what God did to prepare the way for Jesus Christ and the redemption of all who receive Him as Savior and Lord.

STEP 10: Exploring the New Testament

Surveys each of the New Testament books. Shows the essence of the gospel and highlights the exciting beginning of the Christian church.

Leader's Guide

The ultimate resource for even the most inexperienced, timid, and fearful person asked to lead a group study in the basics of the Christian life. Contains questions and answers from the *Ten Basic Steps* Study Guides.

A Handbook for Christian Maturity

Combines the eleven-booklet series into one practical, easy-to-follow volume. Excellent for personal or group study.

Available through your local Christian bookstore, mail-order catalog distributor, or NewLife Publications.

About the Author

BILL BRIGHT is founder and president of Campus Crusade for Christ International. Serving in 152 major countries representing 98 percent of the world's population, he and his dedicated associates of nearly 50,000 full-time staff, associate staff, and trained volunteers have introduced tens of millions of people to Jesus Christ, discipling millions to live Spirit-filled, fruitful lives of purpose and power for the glory of God.

Dr. Bright did graduate study at Princeton and Fuller Theological seminaries from 1946 to 1951. The recipient of many national and international awards, including five honorary doctorates, he is the author of numerous books and publications committed to helping fulfill the Great Commission. His special focus is New Life 2000, an international effort to help reach more than six billion people with the gospel of our Lord Jesus Christ and help fulfill the Great Commission by the year 2000.